Titus Maccius Plautus

Casina

Translation by David Bolton

Published by Lulu Books

2019

Copyright by David Bolton

ISBN 978-0-244-52420-3

Terms for the performance of this play may be obtained from
David Bolton at dgbolton0@gmail.com.

All translations in this edition, including the introductory sections (unless
specifically attributed) are by David Bolton.

Colour: #C3161C

Contents

Titus Maccius Plautus

References in the works of Cicero suggest that Plautus was born c254 BC and died c184 BC. Festus (2nd century AD) says he was born in Sarsina in Umbria in Northern Italy.

Few details of his life are known. There is even doubt about his name: Maccius Plautus could be interpreted as 'Clown Flatfoot'. As to his life, some evidence comes from Aulus Gellius, who, referring to the works of Varro, says "Varro and many others have recorded that he wrote *Saturio*, *Addictus* and a third comedy, the name of which now escapes me, whilst working in a bakery, since, having lost in trade all the money he earned whilst employed in the theatre, he returned destitute to Rome and, to earn a livelihood, he found a job with a baker turning a mill, called a 'hand-mill'."[1] His 'employment in the theatre' presumably would include general work as a stagehand and constructing scenery. His later work in the bakery would have been low-paid, and would have involved operating a mill with two handles, requiring two men to push or turn them. The strength of Gellius' evidence is disputed: it is suggested that the story may have attached itself to Plautus since characters in his plays are often threatened with 'working the mill'. Conversely, of course, this threat could appear frequently in Plautus because of his own personal experience.

Ancient Sarsina was situated in a rural area of North Eastern Italy and Plautus was perhaps unlikely to become acquainted there with either the theatre or, more especially, the Greek theatre. Gellius says of him that 'he returned … to Rome' after his failed commercial venture.

---

[1] Aulus Gellius, *Noctes Atticae* III. 3

How Plautus developed his Latin style, learnt Greek and studied Greek literature is unknown. Perhaps, he left Sarsina for Rome, got caught up in the theatre, and developed the necessary skills in the process.

The twenty-one extant comedies (some being fragmentary) are considered to have been written in the last twenty or twenty-five years of his life, that is, after, say, 209 BC until his death in 184 BC, that is, from around age 45 or 50 to his death at the age of about 70 [1].

The dates of the first performances of most plays, however, are uncertain. *Saturio*, *Addictus* and the third comedy referred to by Gellius appear to have been early works. Gellius adds: "There are about one hundred and thirty comedies ascribed to Plautus, but L. Aelius, a most learned man, judged only twenty-five to be his. But there is no doubt that those that do not seem to have been written by Plautus whilst attributed with his name, were by ancient playwrights, and were reworked and polished by him. Consequently they smack of the Plautine style"[2].

[1] Discussed by G. E. Duckworth, *Nature of Roman Comedy: a Study in Popular Entertainment*

[2] Aulus Gellius, *Noctes Atticae* III. 3

8

Roman comedy

The Greek Old Comedy, performed at the Athenian Dionysia and represented by Aristophanes is associated with the fifth century BC. Little is known of later comedy production until the late fourth century, when Greek New Comedy emerged. The choruses of the earlier Greek plays fell away and dramas took more the format of modern plays. Stock characters emerged: young men in love, slaves cleverer than their masters, female slaves who turn out to be well-born, braggart soldiers, irascible old men who complain about their wives, hungry parasites and greedy slave dealers.

The writers of these comedies include Menander, Philemon and Diphilus of the late fourth and early third centuries. Roman playwrights such as Plautus and Terence took the original plays of these playwrights and did not simply translate them but rewrote them. As Plautus says of the play *Casina*, in its Prologue, "In Greek, the play is called *Clerumenoe*, which means 'The drawing of lots'. Diphilus wrote the play in Greek, and later, Plautus, starting afresh, in Latin". Plautus is known to have reworked the plays of Menander, Philemon, Diphilus and also the minor playwright Demophilus.

Whilst the action of each play takes place in some Greek city (eg. Athens, Sicyon, Epidamnus or Epidaurus), and the actors wore Greek clothes, the references remain Roman: Roman gods, the Roman forum, Rome's magistrates, laws and law courts, the Roman Senate and places in and around Rome.

The Greek clothes of the actors would in particular have included the *pallium* or cloak for the (non-slave) male characters (hence this form of play or *fabula* was called '*palliata*'). Male characters generally wore tunics as the basic item of clothing. There is some debate as to whether masks were worn; being comedy, there would no doubt be some elements of outlandish appearance.

At least part of each play was given musical accompaniment: the surviving texts of the six plays of Terence state that one Flaccus Claudi performed at each first performance of each play on a variety of reed flutes. Commentators have examined the metrical structure of the plays. There is some consensus that some of the dialogue was spoken, but that much of the dialogue and speeches were 'sung', that is, either chanted or sung as recitative to the accompaniment of the flute. There do not appear, however, to have been 'arias' or songs as such.

The plays were performed during Games held as part of religious festivals. The plays of Terence give details of the Games at which his plays were first performed. These include the *Ludi Megalenses* in honour of the Goddess Cybele also known as *Magna Mater*, the *Ludi Romani* in honour of Jupiter, and the Funeral Games held for L. Aemilius Paulus. In other words, they were held at each of the annual *Ludi* and at other one-off important occasions such as a public funeral.

The actors will often have been slaves, who may have been beaten if their performance was poor. They certainly asked for applause at the end of each play. The Epilogue to Plautus' *Cistellaria* (*The Casket*) sums this up:

"Audience, don't expect the actors to appear on stage again: that's the end of the play! They're taking their costumes off now, and the actor who forgot his lines will be given a beating, and the one who didn't will get a drink.

All that remains, is for you, in time honoured fashion, to give us a round of applause."

Roman theatres developed from wooden structures to elaborate stone ones. For the actors, there appear to have been entrances from the wings, a central entrance, and further entrances on either side of the central entrance. This arrangement conveniently fits the set of most Roman comedies, which often present two houses with a street running in front of or between them.

The plays had to appeal to a broad audience. They were studied by literary men such as Varro and Cicero, but they also had to appeal to the Roman populace at large, many of whom would have little or no literary interest, and many of the foreigners in Rome would have little Latin. They also had competition from rival, non-literary performances: Terence tells of the problems he once encountered: "As soon as I began to show it [my play], the challenges of boxers (also the expectation of some tight-rope dancers), the crowds of followers, the noise and the shouts of women, made me finish with the play before the conclusion. I began to apply my old methods to this new play as a trial. I presented it afresh. The first act was well received. Meanwhile, a rumour circulated that a gladiatorial contest was to be held: the crowds gathered; they jostled and shouted and fought for their place."[1]

Yet the Latin of Plautus and Terence is well crafted (though idiomatic) and often in complex verse form. Perhaps, then, it is possible to underestimate the Roman audiences, who must in fact have appreciated the literary aspects of the plays.

[1] Terence, *Hecyra*, Prologus (II)

The broad appeal required of his plays may have led Plautus in particular to be influenced by two earlier Italian theatrical traditions: the Atellane plays and the form of play developed by Livius Andronicus. Livy says that in the mid-fourth century 'scenic games' were introduced; the actors were from Etruria and there were no words but only dancing to the flute; these were imitated locally with the introduction of comic verses and actions to suit the words; this became an accepted form; but then, Livius Andronicus first produced a play with a plot; his plays had spoken dialogue, but also large sections delivered with words 'sung' or chanted to flutes; whilst such plays were left to actors, young men again performed comic verses, known as '*exodia*', or 'after-verses', which were strung together to form 'Atellane plays'; these were of Oscan origin.[1]

St Jerome read Plautus at the end of the fourth century AD; but Plautus received little interest in the Middle Ages, unlike Terence who continued to be copied and read. Plautus resurfaced, however, and influenced Shakespeare, whose *Comedy of Errors* reflects *Menaechmi*, Ben Jonson, whose *The Case is Altered* reflects *Aulularia* and *Captivi*, Molière, whose *L'Avare* is based on *Aulularia*, and many others including Stephen Sondheim's *A Funny Thing Happened on the Way to the Forum* (*Pseudolus*, *Miles Gloriosus* and *Mostellaria*).

[1] Livy, *History of Rome* VII. 2

Casina

As the Prologue tells us, *Casina* is based in a Greek play by Diphilus called '*Clerumenoe*', which means 'The drawing of lots'. Plautus did not so much translate the play as rewrite it in Latin. There appears to be no evidence to identify the date of Diphilus' play, nor of the date of the production of *Casina*. It may be assumed, then, that *Cleroumenoe* was produced a few years either side of 300BC and *Casina* a few years either side of 200BC.

The original Greek play was set in Athens and Plautus retained this setting for *Casina*. Whilst the play is intended to reflect the lively Greek culture, Roman audiences would appreciate references to the Senate, the forum, Hannibal's elephants and Roman lawyers.

Casina contains many of the stock characters of Roman comedy: Lycidamus and Alcesimus are old men who complain about their wives and Lycidamus looks for a younger alternative. Cleostrata and Myrrhina are the wives complained about and they are happy to seek revenge. Olympio and Pardalisca in particular are slaves always capable of outwitting their master. The other slaves provide slapstick interludes.

The set of *Casina*, as was common in Roman comedies, featured two houses with a street running in front of or between them.

The opening remarks of the Prologue do not form part of the play and perhaps would be varied from performance to performance to suit the circumstances. The later part of the Prologue is typical of Roman comedy: it sets the scene, ensures the audience understand at the outset what the play is about, and enables the playwright to launch straight into the plot – thus capturing and maintaining the interest of a possibly fickle audience.

The characters names are derived from Greek, and in some cases have amusing derivations: 'Chalinus', for example, means a horse's bit or combined bit and bridle.

The characters Lysidamus and Citrio, the cook, are not named in the text, nor are they referred to by name in the course of the dialogue. Most manuscripts refer to Lysidamus simply as 'Senex' ie. 'Old man'. 'Lysidamus' was written on the scene headings of one text produced five hundred years after Plautus' death and has been used ever since.[1]

A problem for Plautus was that Roman slaves did not enter into formal marriages. To overcome any confusion with his Roman audience, he points out in the Prologue that slaves did marry – in Greece and Carthage and in Apulia.

---

[1] *Greek and Roman Comedy*, Edited by Shawn O'Bryhim, University of Texas Press

Casina

(The Plot and the Dramatis Personae set out on pages 17 and 19 derive from the transmitted editions of the play.)

The Plot [1]

Competing for a slave girl are two slaves;
A father champions one, and one the son.
Success is to the father; yet he's fooled:
In girl's disguise, a slave – a worthless man –
Next comes, to thrash both master and his man.
A citizen proved, Casina weds the son.

[1] The Plot is thought not to have been written by Plautus.

Dramatis Personae[1]

Olympio ⎫
            ⎬ slaves
Chalinus ⎭

Cleostrata,   a married woman

Pardalisca,   a slave girl

Myrrhina,   a married woman

Lysidamus ⎫
            ⎬ old men
Alcesimus ⎭

A Cook

---

[1] The Prologue is spoken by a member of the cast; Olympio, slave of Lysidamus, a farm manager; Chalinus, slave of Lysidamus' son; Cleostrata, wife of Lysidamus; Pardalisca, slave girl of Cleostrata; Myrrhina, wife of Alcesimus; Lysidamus, an old man; Alcesimus, an old man; Citrio, a cook, slave of Lysidamus; the Epilogue is spoken by a member of the cast.

Casina

Scene: Athens; the houses of Lysidamus and Alcesimus face on to the street.

PROLOGUE

Welcome most excellent audience! You prize Good Faith: and so I welcome Good Faith also. And having welcomed Good Faith, I know from the outset that you will be fair-minded about our play.

Wise men, I think, drink old wine, and happily watch old plays. You enjoy the works and words of ancient times, and so it's right that you should enjoy old plays beyond all others. Some of the modern comedies can't hold a candle to them.

Now, popular rumour tells us there is a demand for the plays of Plautus; and so we present a comedy of his – an ancient one. The play was popular amongst the audiences of the time, although we know that today's audiences may not have come across it. But we shall do our utmost to make you all appreciate it.

When it was first performed, it outshone all the plays of the day. That was a time of flourishing playwrights, who now, of course, have passed away. Yet, in their passing, they leave their benefits for the audiences of today.

I therefore beg that you kindly give your attention to our troupe of actors and that you cast from your minds all your cares and debts – there are no debt collectors here! We can be light-hearted: the banks don't know the meaning of the word, but they are now closed and business is done for the day.

And so, now that you have nothing else on your mind, please pay attention to me: I would like to give you the name of our comedy. In Greek, the play is called '*Clerumenoe*', which means '*The Drawing of Lots*'. Diphilus wrote the play in Greek, and later, Plautus, starting afresh, in Latin.

And so…
An old married man lives around here. He has a son, who, together with his father, lives in that house there (*indicating Lysidamas' house*). He has a slave who lies in sickness – or rather, to tell the truth, he lies in bed. Early one morning sixteen years before our play begins, just along this street, at daybreak, this slave saw a woman abandoning a baby girl. He approached her and asked her to give him the baby, which she did. The slave brought the baby home, here, gave her to his mistress, and asked her to care for the baby. She agreed and brought the child up as if she were her own daughter. Well, not quite. She took the opportunity to bring the girl up as a slave, working as a maid in her house.

By the time of our play, the child has become the most beautiful girl in Athens: nubile, curvaceous, voluptuous – you know the kind of thing. She has certainly not escaped the notice of the old man. She has also failed to escape the notice of the old man's son. Both father and son are drawing up their battle plans to seize the opportunities presented by the presence of this beautiful girl in their house. To begin with, neither of them is aware that they are mutual rivals.

The son isn't thinking of marrying the girl – as a slave, she's far too far down the social ladder. The old man *is* thinking of marrying the girl, but has the misfortune, as he sees it, to be married already.

But why should the trivial detail of a social ladder or being married already get in the way of these two men's plans? They each have their own solutions.

The father's plan is this: he has a slave who acts as his farm manager. He has persuaded this slave to ask to marry the girl. 'Doesn't that rather defeat the object?' you ask – particularly as the farm manager, is extremely keen on the idea. Clearly you are not used to owning slaves. The old man knows that slaves do as they are told – by bribery…. or by force – and that the girl married to his slave leaves all avenues open to himself. The old man has chosen this slave carefully: he lives on the old man's farm out in the country – well away from the old man's wife.

The son has had a similar idea: he is in the army and has a slave who accompanies him on his military duties. He has given this slave the job of marrying the girl, (a job which he accepts entirely willingly). The son knows this slave is also not immune to bribery or force, and if the son's slave marries the girl, the son's path to the girl will be wide open.

The old man's wife has discovered he is pursuing a love affair. And in this particular piece of father-son rivalry, she is completely clear that her son is to win and her husband is to lose.

But after a while, the old man realises he and his son are pursuing the same girl. Fearing his plans may be thwarted, he has packed his son off abroad. Of course, he won't defeat his wife as easily as that, but the son will not return before the end of the play. He tries to, but Plautus doesn't want him to and makes a bridge collapse that lies on his way home. His mother therefore is left to defeat the old man by herself.

There may be some pedants amongst you who say "By Hercules, slaves do not marry!" Well, they do in parts of Greece and in Carthage …and in Apulia. Ask any Greek or Carthaginian or Apulian!

So, let us return to our beautiful young girl, whom two slaves, are doing their best to marry. She will prove to be chaste, free and a native Athenian; and no dishonour will attach to her – well, not in this play. After the play, she'll no doubt be as keen to marry for money as the rest of you ladies...

But enough! Let us now proceed with our play! I bid you all farewell.

ACT 1

(*Enter* Olympio *from along the street. He looks angry. Enter* Chalinus *from along the street, following him close behind.*)

OLYMPIO Look! I can mind my own business without you watching over me. All right? So what do you think you're doing following me about, anyway?

CHALINUS I've come to realise I need to shadow you night and day, wherever you go. In fact, I'd follow you all the way to the hangman!

So think about it, Olympio. I know you're a tricky character, but am I really going to let you butt in and take Casina from under my nose? Do you think I'm going to let you marry Casina? I know you'd like to, but from now on, I'm going to make sure I know every move you make.

OLYMPIO What I do is nothing to do with you.

CHALINUS What's that! You've a nerve! Why are you sneaking about the city anyway? You're supposed to be running a farm.

OLYMPIO Because I feel like it.

CHALINUS Well, why aren't you back in your farmyard where you belong? Why aren't you doing the job you've been given, and leave off matters in the city? Casina's engaged to me. So don't you come round here to steal her. Clear off back to your farm – back to where you belong!

OLYMPIO I have not forgotten my duties at the farm, Chalinus. I have left someone in charge who will look after it quite properly.

Now, once I've got from the city what I came for...,
once I've married that girl you've got your eyes on, the sweet and tender Casina, your fellow slave...,

25

once I've taken her back to the farm..., then I'll be bedded in... where I belong.

CHALINUS You! Marry her! I'd hang myself before I saw you get control of her!

OLYMPIO You might as well get your noose ready then! She's mine.

CHALINUS Oh she's yours is she. Do you really think she'll want to marry an unwashed muck-spreader like you?

OLYMPIO You know the score.

CHALINUS You'll regret it!

OLYMPIO As slaves go, Chalinus, you're the lowest of the low. And you can rest assured my wedding will give me plenty of opportunities to make your life not worth living.

CHALINUS Such as?

OLYMPIO First of all, in case you're in any doubt about who's marrying Casina, you'll attend on us at our wedding.

After this honour, you will attend on us at the farm and you will be reduced to your usual vile and good-for-nothing servility; you'll work your fingers to the bone; you'll fetch and carry and you'll work from morn till night like the grovelling slave you are. You will eat animal fodder, or dirt like a worm; and if you don't, you'll return to the farm worn out and starved. At night, when you're tired and famished, I'll make sure you have somewhere very suitable to sleep.

CHALINUS Oh yes?

OLYMPIO You shall sleep outside our window and there you'll lay while I lay Casina. And when she says 'My Olympio, my darling, my life, my everything' – and all the other things women say on these occasions –

then you, you wretch of a slave, will be consumed with endless jealousy.

Now don't bother to reply; your conversation's rather boring.

(*Exit* Olympio *into Lysidamus' house*)

CHALINUS I'll follow. I'll make sure (*as if talking to the departed Olympio*) you don't do anything without my keeping an eye on you.

(*Exit* Chalinus *into Lysidamus' house.*)

ACT 2

(*Enter* Cleostrata *and* Pardalisca *from Lysidamus' house*)

CLEOSTRATA   (*to servants within*) Maids, lock up the
    stores and bring the key to me. I'm going round to
    my next door neighbour's. If my husband should
    want me for anything, come round for me.
PARDALISCA   Master said lunch was to be prepared for
    him.
CLEOSTRATA Sh! Be quiet and go away.

(*Exit* Pardalisca *into Lysidamus' house*)

CLEOSTRATA I shall have no lunch prepared, nor will any
    food be cooked today, whilst that man chases after
    his women and rides roughshod over me and his own
    son – the disgrace that he is.
    I'll get my own back on that womaniser. He can go
    without food and drink. And he'll get the rough side
    of my tongue. His life will be a misery. By the Gods,
    I can be properly unpleasant when I want to be! From
    now on, he'll lead the life he deserves – that
    debauched, evil, lump of flesh that's supposed to be
    my husband.
    So, now I'm going next door to complain to my
    neighbour about the way I'm being treated.

(*The door of Alcesimus' house begins to open*)

CLEOSTRATA Ah, but her door's opening – and here she
    is coming out.

[2.2]
(*Enter* Myrrhina *from Alcesimus' house*)

MYRRHINA (*to maids within*) Girls, you're to come next
    door with me.
    (*after a slight pause*) Is there anyone who is listening
    to what I'm saying? I shall be next door if my
    husband or anyone wants me.
    (*aside*) When I'm in the house on my own, I can't
    keep my eyes open, let alone get on with any work.
    (*to maids within*) Didn't I say to bring my spinning?!
CLEOSTRATA Good morning, Myrrhina.
MYRRHINA Good morning, but, tell me, why are you
    looking so upset?
CLEOSTRATA Oh, I'm having an absolutely awful day:
    it's the usual marital problems, I'm afraid. There's
    always something going wrong.
    Anyway, I was just coming round to see you.
MYRRHINA And I was just coming round to see you.
    But what is it that's particularly troubling you at the
    moment. You know that what troubles you troubles
    me too.
CLEOSTRATA I can see now why I love you more than
    any other of my neighbours: you do help me more
    than anyone else.
MYRRHINA And I love you and that's why I'm trying to
    find out what's happened.
CLEOSTRATA I'm pushed to one side in my own home.
    My husband thinks he can walk all over me.
MYRRHINA Now come on: tell me exactly what's going
    on.
CLEOSTRATA My husband takes me for granted, and I've
    no choice in matters where I ought to have a choice.

MYRRHINA   That's strange, if what you say is true. It's usually men who say they can't get their own way even though they are always right.

CLEOSTRATA   Well: I have girl. She's mine: I've paid for her upbringing. Well, he wants to marry her to his farm manager, against my will. The reality is he loves her himself.

MYRRHINA   I think you should keep your voice down.

CLEOSTRATA   Oh, we can talk here; we are alone.

MYRRHINA   So we are. Where did you get her? Of course, the perfect wife does not have property of her own unbeknown to her husband: and, quite frankly, if she does, she has either taken it from him or earned it dishonourably. I must say, in my opinion, I must say, in my opinion, whatever is yours does also belong to your husband.

CLEOSTRATA   You're criticizing me as well, in everything you say.

MYRRHINA   Be quiet, silly, and listen to me.
Don't go against him. Let him have his affairs; let him do as he pleases – so long as you lack nothing at home.

CLEOSTRATA   Are you in your right mind? You wouldn't really want that for yourself, would you?

MYRRHINA   Not really, but remember our divorce laws, my dear. We women don't stand a chance. A husband only has to say "Go outside, woman," and he's half-way to divorcing you. Now, we don't want any of that, do we?

CLEOSTRATA   Sh! Keep quiet.

MYRRHINA   What's wrong?

CLEOSTRATA   (*pointing down the street*) There!

MYRRHINA   Who is it?

30

CLEOSTRATA My husband's coming. Go inside, quick!
    Hurry, please!
MYRRHINA All right, I'm going.
CLEOSTRATA Soon, when you and I have a little more
    time, I need to talk to you. Goodbye for now.
MYRRHINA Goodbye.

(*Exit* Myrrhina *into Alcesimus' house; Cleostrata stands
unseen in her doorway.*)

[2.3]
(*Enter* Lysidamus *along the street. His clothes are comically
dishevelled and he carries a wine flask. He is clearly drunk.*)

LYSIDAMUS   Yes, I do believe that love surpasses
    everything, even the most splendid splendidness. It is
    impossible to name anything which makes life more
    agreeable or gives it greater flavour than love. You
    know, how surprising it is that cooks, who use so
    many spices, do not use this one spice which excels
    them all. Now who can resist a dish which is spiced
    with love? And no food can be truly smooth and
    flavoursome if it does not have love as an ingredient.
    Even the bitterest herb is made honey-sweet by love.
    Love turns the most miserable man to a man
    (*signifying himself*) who is elegant and gentle. Of
    course, I need no-one to tell me all this: I speak from
    personal experience. Since I fell in love with Casina,
    how I feel myself blossoming. Elegance herself has
    no finer bloom. I visit all the perfumeries and when I
    find a pleasing perfume, I perfume myself – to please
    her. And I do please her, I'm sure of it.
    But my wife gets on my nerves - by being alive.

(*sees Cleostrata*) Oh dear! I can see her standing there with that disagreeable look. Well, I'd better treat the miserable object to a bit of flattery:
(*He moves towards Cleostrata and attempts to kiss her. As he holds his arms out to embrace her, he is still holding his wine flask.*)
My dear and delightful wife, how is everything?

CLEOSTRATA (*pushing him away abruptly*) Take your hands off me!

LYSIDAMUS (*still attempting to kiss her*) But surely my Juno is not annoyed with her Jupiter.

CLEOSTRATA Let me go! (*making to go indoors*)

LYSIDAMUS Wait a moment!

CLEOSTRATA No!

LYSIDAMUS By the Gods, I'll follow you! (*continues to attempt to kiss her*)

CLEOSTRATA You're mad!

LYSIDAMUS Madly in love with you!

CLEOSTRATA Well don't be!

LYSIDAMUS Can't help it!

CLEOSTRATA You'll be the death of me!

LYSIDAMUS (*aside*) If only...

CLEOSTRATA I heard that!

LYSIDAMUS Look at me, my sweet.

CLEOSTRATA (*sniffing at Lysidamus*) You're the sweet one. What on earth is that perfume smell?

LYSIDAMUS (*turning away*) Oh disaster! Caught red-handed! Can I wipe it off with my cloak? I hope the Gods burn that perfume shop down, for giving me that stuff!

CLEOSTRATA Oh, you useless fool! Just what kind of picture do you think you're presenting? – a man of your age walking through the streets lathered in perfume?

LYSIDAMUS (*positively but unconvincingly*) A friend of mine…. was buying the perfume: I was just helping him.

CLEOSTRATA You made that up quickly. Aren't you ashamed?

LYSIDAMUS (*sarcastically*) Yes. Deeply.

CLEOSTRATA And where's that (*lowering her voice*) – whore-house – you've been visiting?

LYSIDAMUS Whore-house? Who, me?

CLEOSTRATA I know more than you think.

LYSIDAMUS Do you? What do you know?

CLEOSTRATA I know there are plenty of stupid old men, but you're the stupidest. So! Where have you been, you useless imbecile? Where do you go? Where's that whore-house? Where do you go drinking? By the Gods, you're drunk! Look how your cloak's creased.

LYSIDAMUS May the Gods strike me – and you - down with a thunderbolt, if I've allowed one drop of wine to pass my lips today. (*cowers in expectation.*)

CLEOSTRATA Go on; do as you please: eat, drink, ruin us all.

LYSIDAMUS Right! That's enough! Calm yourself: you've rattled on too long. Save your speech-making for tomorrow if you want to carry on arguing. Well now, have you cooled down enough to let your husband have his way on a certain matter?

CLEOSTRATA What matter?

LYSIDAMUS Kind of you to ask. (*putting down his wine flask*) The matter of the slave-girl, Casina. Is she to be married to Olympio, our worthy farm manager, where she will have plenty of wood, hot water, food and clothes and where she can bring up her children comfortably? Or is she to be wed to that worthless slave, Chalinus, who is both useless and dishonest and who so far hasn't a lead drachma to his name?

CLEOSTRATA Well, I'm surprised at you. You've clearly forgotten how to behave – and at your time of life.

LYSIDAMUS Meaning what?

CLEOSTRATA If you were to do what was right and proper, you would allow me to look after the slave-girls. They are my responsibility.

LYSIDAMUS How could you possibly give her to that shield-carrying fellow, that slave of our son's?

CLEOSTRATA Because we ought to help our only son.

LYSIDAMUS Only son! He might be my only son, but I'm his only father. And my wishes should take precedence.

CLEOSTRATA By the Gods, you're up to no good!

LYSIDAMUS (*aside*) I think she may suspect something. (*aloud*) N-no good, did you say?

CLEOSTRATA Why are you stammering? You seem very eager for something.

LYSIDAMUS I simply want her to marry a slave who is worthy rather than one who is worthless.

CLEOSTRATA But what if I manage to persuade your slave Olympio to allow Casina to marry our son's slave, Chalinus?

LYSIDAMUS Well, what if I manage to persuade our son's slave Chalinus to allow Casina to marry my slave, Olympio? I'm sure I'd succeed.

CLEOSTRATA Very well. Do you want me to call Chalinus out here for you to talk to? You speak to him and I'll speak to your farm manager.

LYSIDAMUS Go ahead.

CLEOSTRATA He'll be here in a moment. This will test our powers of persuasion.

(*Exit* Cleostrata *into Lysidamus' house, leaving the door open*)

LYSIDAMUS May all the Gods destroy that woman! I can speak now she's gone. Here am I, excruciatingly love-sick, whilst she makes a point of opposing everything I do.

(*Enter* Chalinus *unseen at Lysidamus' doorway*)

LYSIDAMUS She suspects my plans. Yes, that's why she's going out of her way to help Chalinus – may the Gods destroy him!

[2.4]
CHALINUS You called me, so your wife tells me.
LYSIDAMUS Yes, I ordered for you to be called.
CHALINUS Say what you want.
LYSIDAMUS First of all, I'd like you to look a little more cheerful when you talk to me. It's rather foolish to grimace at someone who, as it happens, has power over you.
Now Chalinus, for some time now, I have thought you to be an upright, worthy fellow....
CHALINUS I understand. If you think that, why not set me free from my slavery?
LYSIDAMUS I want to; but my wanting to means nothing – unless you help by doing something for me.
CHALINUS All I need to know is what you want me to do.
LYSIDAMUS Listen and I'll tell you. It's Casina: I promised to have her married to Olympio, my farm manager.
CHALINUS But your wife and son promised her to me.

35

LYSIDAMUS I know; but would you prefer to be a free bachelor, or to spend your life a married slave – and for your children to be slaves? The choice is yours. Those are my terms.

CHALINUS If I were to be free, I would live my life at my own expense: now I live it at yours. As for Casina, one thing is certain: I'll give her up to no man alive.

LYSIDAMUS Go inside this instant and tell my wife to come out here immediately. (*Chalinus turns to go indoors.*) And fill an urn with water and bring it out here along with two round pebbles so that we can draw lots.

CHALINUS (*moving back to face Lysidamus*) Ah! You want to draw lots, eh? That suits me.

LYDIDAMUS By the Gods, I'll settle this conspiracy one way or the other. If I can't succeed by persuasion, then I'm prepared to take my chance. And I'll have my revenge on you and your supporters. (*walking away from Chalinus*)

CHALINUS Except that I'm going to win.

LYSIDAMUS (*aside*) Well, his number's up, certainly.

CHALINUS She'll marry me, in spite of all your planning and plotting.

LYSIDAMUS Leave my sight, will you!

CHALINUS You obviously don't like the look of me. Never mind; I'll survive.

(*Exit* Chalinus *into Lysidamus' house*)

LYSIDAMUS What a miserable situation! Everything conspires to thwart me! My fear now is that my wife succeeds in persuading my slave, Olympio, not to marry Casina. If that happens, then I'm completely done for. Only if my wife fails, is there any hope in drawing the lots. But if the lots go against me, I shall make my sword my bed and lay me down upon it!

(*Lysidamus' door opens and through it: Enter* Olympio)

LYSIDAMUS But here comes Olympio. Excellent!

[2.5]
OLYMPIO (*to Cleostrata within*) By the Gods, madam, you might as well push me into a hot oven and bake me brown as bread as try to persuade me to do that!
LYSIDAMUS (*aside*) Saved! His words suggest my hopes are intact.
OLYMPIO (*to Cleostrata within*) Why do you threaten me, madam, with your talk of liberty? You and your son know as well as I do that, whether you two like it or not, I could free myself from slavery for a couple of drachmas.

(*Olympio closes the door and comes out.*)

LYSIDAMUS What's going on? Who were you arguing with?
OLYMPIO Why? Who do you always argue with?
LYSIDAMUS My wife, then?
OLYMPIO Wife? You call her a wife? You're like a hunter in the wild – you spend your days and nights with a dog!
LYSIDAMUS What's her line? What's she been saying to you?
OLYMPIO She's begging me not to marry Casina.
LYSIDAMUS And your reply?
OLYMPIO I said Jupiter couldn't persuade me to give her up – not if he begged me.

LYSIDAMUS May the Gods preserve you!

OLYMPIO Now she's becoming so over-heated, I think she'll reach boiling point soon.

LYSIDAMUS Do you think she might disappear in a cloud of steam?

OLYMPIO Well she might. However, the truth is your love affair has become troublesome for me. Your wife's hostile towards me; your son's hostile; your whole household's hostile.

LYSIDAMUS What concern is that of yours? Whilst ever (*indicating himself*) Jupiter, in the form of myself here, is on your side, those (*indicating those in his house*) lesser deities count for nothing.

OLYMPIO You jest! As if you didn't know, human Jupiters tend to die off suddenly. Now tell me this: if Jupiter here (*indicating Lysidamus*) were to die, and the lesser deities were to inherit his kingdom, who's going to prevent me from getting a flogging?

LYSIDAMUS But you'd be better off than you think, if we succeed and I get to bed with Casina.

OLYMPIO By Hercules, I don't think there's much chance of that, with your wife taking such pains to prevent her marrying me.

LYSIDAMUS Right! This is what I'm going to do: I'm going to have you and Chalinus draw lots for Casina. I can see from events that the time has come to draw swords and fight to the bitter end!

OLYMPIO What if the draw doesn't go the way you want?

LYSIDAMUS Don't tempt fate! Let's rely on the Gods for help.

OLYMPIO That's cold comfort! We mere mortals all have to rely on the gods; but the 'Let's rely on the gods brigade' have come to grief often enough.

(*Lysidamus' door opens*)

LYSIDAMUS Sh! Quiet a moment!
OLYMPIO Why?

(*Enter* Chalinus *through the doorway, carrying an urn and two round pebbles for lots. Then: Enter* Cleostrata *carrying a jug of water.*)

LYSIDAMUS Look, here comes Chalinus with the urn and the lots. Now we'll engage battle and fight to the finish.

[2.6]
(*Cleostrata stands by Chalinus.*)

CLEOSTRATA Chalinus, tell me what my husband wants
    of me.
CHALINUS I think he wants you dead and gone, to be quite
    honest.
CLEOSTRATA You know, I think he does!
CHALINUS I don't think; I know!
LYSIDAMUS (*aside*) Some slaves are brighter than you'd
    think: this one here's a mind reader.
    (*to Olympio, as if a military commander*) All right
    men! Let's raise our standard and engage the enemy!
    Follow me.
    (*Lysidamus followed by Olympio crosses to Chalinus
    and Cleostrata, whom he addresses.*)
    What are you two doing?
CHALINUS Everything you ordered is here: wife, lots, urn
    and myself.
OLYMPIO (*to Chalinus*) Well, you're surplus to
    requirements for a start.
CHALINUS That's your view, of course. You'll regret
    engaging me in battle – I'll strike a blow that breaks

39

your heart. Look, you're afraid – you're sweating already.

LYSIDAMUS Quiet, Chalinus!

(*Olympio prepares to hit Chalinus*)

CHALINUS Keep him off !

(*Lysidamus intervenes.*)

OLYMPIO Watch your step, Chalinus!

LYSIDAMUS (*to* Chalinus) Now put the urn here (*indicating a recess in the house wall*) and give me the lots.

(*Chalinus gives the lots to Lysidamus.*)

Pay attention everyone.

(*to Cleostrata*) I was of the opinion, Cleostrata, that I could have persuaded you to let me have my way in this matter and that you would have allowed Casina to become my wife. And I still feel ……

CLEOSTRATA Become *your* wife!?

LYSIDAMUS My wife… Aaa! I didn't mean to say that. When I wanted to say 'my', I said 'his'… and whilst I myself desire… no, that's wrong. By Hercules, I've been talking complete rubbish…..

CLEOSTRATA And you still are!

LYSIDAMUS He… no, I … Just a moment, I think I'm back on the right track….

CLEOSTRATA That will certainly be an improvement.

LYSIDAMUS These things happen when you get excited. Now, I recognize that you have a say in all this, and we both, that is Olympio and myself, appeal to you.

CLEOSTRATA Meaning?

LYSIDAMUS I mean to ask this, my dearest: In the case of Casina, please do Olympio a favour.

CLEOSTRATA By the Gods, I'll do him no favours nor allow anyone else to.

LYSIDAMUS In that case, shall I now prepare the lottery?

CLEOSTRATA Who's stopping you?

(Lysidamus takes the jug of water from Cleostrata and pours the water into the urn.)

LYSIDAMUS   This tried and tested method of deciding disputes is undoubtedly the best and the fairest. If the result is as we want, we shall rejoice. If it is otherwise, we shall accept it with equanimity.
(to Olympio) You take this lot.
(Lysidamus gives one lot to Olympio.)
See what's written on it.
OLYMPIO *(reading)* Number one.
CHALINUS Hey! Why has he got the first one?
LYSIDAMUS *(to Chalinus)* And you take this one.
CHALINUS *(taking it suspiciously)* All right.
(slowly) Just a minute! *(to Cleostrata)* Just check that there isn't another lot in there under the water.
LYSIDAMUS   You insolent slave! We're not all like you, you know!
CLEOSTRATA *(checking)* There isn't one, rest assured.
CHALINUS *(stands forward ready to cast his lot into the urn)* May the Gods be favourable to me.
OLYMPIO   Oh how pious! I don't think the Gods will be too concerned about the likes of you! But just a minute; you haven't got a lot made out of wood have you?
CHALINUS Why?
OLYMPIO Because I don't want yours floating on top of the water.
LYSIDAMUS   Get ready! Throw your lots in the urn – Now!
(Olympio and Chalinus drop their lots into the urn.)
Cleostrata, check there are two lots in the urn.

41

OLYMPIO Don't trust your wife.
LYSIDAMUS Courage, Olympio!

(*Cleostrata checks the urn and stirs the water with her hand*)

OLYMPIO   By Hercules, the witch'll put a spell on those
    lots if she touches them!
LYSIDAMUS Be quiet!
OLYMPIO   I am quiet. (*seriously, standing as to pray*) I
    pray the Gods ….
CHALINUS …that you'll spend your life in chains!
OLYMPIO …that my lot will win.
CHALINUS ….that your lot will be to hang by the feet!
OLYMPIO ….and that you'll blow your eyes through your
    nose!
CHALINUS You look nervous. Afraid of losing?
OLYMPIO You're dead!
LYSIDAMUS Pay attention, both of you.
OLYMPIO It's not me who's making a noise.
LYSIDAMUS Now, Cleostrata, I don't want you to be able
    to claim there was any cheating by me going on here,
    or even to have any suspicions.
    Therefore, I'll let you draw the winning lot yourself.
OLYMPIO   (*to Lysidamus, suspecting Cleostrata of
    cheating*) Are you trying to ruin my life?
CHALINUS He'd even make money out of that.
CLEOSTRATA I should think so.
CHALINUS I pray the Gods…that your lot disappears from
    the urn altogether.
OLYMPIO   Yes, you know all about disappearing acts,
    don't you, particularly when there's some work to do.
CHALINUS You'll disappear soon enough if I get hold of a
    whip!
LYSIDAMUS Olympio, let's get on with this, shall we?

OLYMPIO If this clown will let us.

LYSIDAMUS May good fortune be with me!

OLYMPIO Don't you mean 'with me'?

CHALINUS No, he means 'with me'.

CLEOSTRATA *(to Olympio, indicating Chalinus)* Yes, he'll win and you've had it!

(Chalinus pushes Olympio, with a laugh.)

LYSIDAMUS *(to Olympio)* What! Break his jaw for him! Come on then!

(Chalinus takes guard.)

OLYMPIO Shall I punch him or just slap him?

LYSIDAMUS Please yourself.

(to Chalinus, who is preparing to fight) You, keep your hands to yourself! *(Chalinus drops his guard)*

OLYMPIO Right! *(punching Chalinus on the jaw)*

CLEOSTRATA What do you think you're doing?

OLYMPIO *(indicating Lysidamus)* Jupiter told me to do it.

CLEOSTRATA *(to Chalinus)* Go hit him back!

(Chalinus strikes Olympio with a combination of punches to the head.)

OLYMPIO Jupiter! He's punching me to death!

LYSIDAMUS *(to Chalinus)* Stop that! What do you think you're doing?

CHALINUS *(indicating Cleostrata)* Juno told me to do it.

LYSIDAMUS *(about to remonstrate with Cleostrata but thinking better of it)* Yes, well, Cleostrata likes to be obeyed.

CLEOSTRATA Chalinus has as much right to speak as Olympio.

OLYMPIO I was looking for good luck and he spoilt it.

LYSIDAMUS Yes, don't go looking for trouble, Chalinus.

CHALINUS He waits till I've been punched on the jaw to tell me that.

LYSIDAMUS Now then, Cleostrata, draw the winning lot. Pay attention you two!

(*aside*) I'm so nervous I don't know where I am: I can't bear it. My heart's beating so loudly inside my chest, I think I'm going to have a heart attack.

CLEOSTRATA (*putting her hand in the urn*) I've got one.

LYSIDAMUS Bring it out!

CHALINUS (*to a worried looking Olympio*) Are you dead yet?

(*Cleostrata draws the winning lot. Olympio pushes forward.*)

OLYMPIO Show us it!

(*Cleostrata holds it up for all to see.*)

OLYMPIO It's mine! Yes!

CHALINUS What!!

CLEOSTRATA (*checks the lot*) You've lost, Chalinus.

LYSIDAMUS (*engages in victory dance*) The Gods were on our side, Olympio! Magnificent!

OLYMPIO (*exultant, mocking Chalinus*) It's all down to piety, you know – mine and my ancestors.

LYSIDAMUS (*exultant and impatient*) Go inside, Cleostrata, and prepare the wedding!

CLEOSTRATA I shall do as you say.

LYSIDAMUS Well, you know it's a long way to his farmhouse, where he's to take her?

CLEOSTRATA Yes

LYSIDAMUS Well, go on then, inside. And however much all this irritates you, make sure you organize it properly.

CLEOSTRATA I will.

(*Exit* Cleostrata *into Lysidamus' house.*)

LYSIDAMUS (*to Olympio*) Let's go inside as well. We can put some pressure on them all to hurry up.

OLYMPIO I'm not holding you up, am I?

LYSIDAMUS (*quietly to Olympio*) No; it's just that I don't want to talk any more in front of him (*indicating Chalinus*).

(*Exeunt* Lysidamus *and* Olympio *into Lysidamus' house*)

[2.7]

CHALINUS If I were to hang myself now, firstly, I would have wasted all my efforts, secondly, I would have the expense of buying a rope and thirdly, I would be pleasing my enemies. On the other hand, does it matter if I am dead?

Anyway, I was defeated in the drawing of lots and Casina is to marry the farm manager. Now it's not this – being beaten by the farm manager – that's really upsetting me, so much as the enormous effort on the part of the old man to ensure that I didn't marry her and that Olympio did. To think how agitated he was and what a stew he got himself into; and how he jumped and danced about when that fool Olympio won.

(*Lysidamus' door begins to open*)

Ah! The door's opening. I'll move out of the way here. (*withdraws out of sight of the door.*)

(*Enter* Olympio, *wearing the white tunic of a bridegroom, and* Lysidamus *from Lysidamus' house.*)

CHALINUS (*sarcastically*) My friends and benefactors are coming out. An ambush! Yes, I'll ambush them from here.

[2.8]

OLYMPIO Just let him come out to the farm! I'll truss him up like a chicken and send him back to town.

LYSIDAMUS I should hope you would.

OLYMPIO Yes, I can take care of him.

LYSIDAMUS If Chalinus had been at home, I wanted to send him with you to buy the food for your wedding. There's nothing like kicking a man when he's down.

CHALINUS (*throughout this scene, talking to himself and the audience*) I'll imitate a crab and move backwards to the wall. I can overhear their conversation from here. One wants to crucify me; the other wants to tenderise me afterwards. Look at him, walking about in his white wedding outfit and looking very pleased with himself: a good flogging wouldn't go amiss! I'm postponing my death; one thing is definite – I'm sending him to Hades first.

OLYMPIO (*to Lysidamus*) Well, I've certainly proved accommodating, and the greatest object of your desire will soon be yours. You will soon have what you want, without your wife knowing.

LYSIDAMUS Don't tell everyone! By the Gods, I'm so happy I want to kiss you, Olympio! (*referring to Casina*) Yes, the greatest object of my desire! (*holds his arms out to embrace Olympio*)

CHALINUS Kiss him! Greatest object of his desire! Is he going to give him one!

OLYMPIO You approve of me now?

LYSIDAMUS Olympio, you are my number one! May I embrace you?

CHALINUS 'Embrace him', now, is it?

OLYMPIO If you want.

(*Lysidamus moves forward to embrace Olympio.*)

LYSIDAMUS Oh, this is like tasting honey!

(*As Lysidamus advances, Olympio recoils and turns his back on Lysidamus.*)

OLYMPIO I know you're keen, but get yourself off my back!

(*Lysidamus does so, with an appearance of reluctance.*)

CHALINUS Ah, so that's the reason he promoted him to farm manager! And he offered me the job of steward. Good job I turned that down!

OLYMPIO How obliging I've been today; how I've made your day!

LYSIDAMUS And how I'll spend my life thinking more of you than I do of myself.

CHALINUS By Hercules, he'll be getting his leg over any minute. The old man always did like men with beards.

LYSIDAMUS Ah, I shall soon be kissing Casina: Oh, I'm looking forward to a whale of a time – without my wife knowing.

CHALINUS Oh, I've been getting it wrong – but I've got it right now! It's Casina he's after. I've got these two now!

LYSIDAMUS I'm just longing to hug her, to kiss her!

OLYMPIO I'm to be her husband, actually. Shouldn't I take her home first? Don't be in such a hurry.

LYSIDAMUS But I'm in love.

OLYMPIO But I don't think it can be arranged today.

LYSIDAMUS It can. Particularly if you think you are going to be set free from slavery tomorrow.

CHALINUS I can see my ears are going to have to be at their sharpest, since it seems I will have a golden opportunity to kill two birds with one stone.

LYSIDAMUS And a place is ready for me at the home of a friend and neighbour of mine. I've confided in him - all about my affair with Casina: and he said he'd let me have the use of his house.

OLYMPIO What about his wife? Where will she be?

LYSIDAMUS We've got round that neatly. My wife is going to invite her round to our house for the wedding. She's a friend willing to help and she'll spend the night at our house. I told my wife to ask her and she agreed. So my friend's wife will be here (*indicating his own house*) and I'll ensure her husband's away from home. You'll be taking your wife to the farm, except that the farm will be there (*indicating Alcesimus' house*) for as long as I'm with Casina 'celebrating her marriage'. Then you take her early in the morning to the real farm. Pretty clever, eh?

OLYMPIO Well worked out.

CHALINUS Too clever by half, I think you'll find.

LYSIDAMUS Do you know what to do now?

OLYMPIO No, tell me.

LYSIDAMUS Take this purse. Go and buy something for Casina and me to eat – some fine delicacies, since she's something of a delicacy herself.

OLYMPIO Fine

LYSIDAMUS Buy some cuttle-fish in barley.

CHALINUS Or perhaps just some bread and water.

LYSIDAMUS Buy some sole.

CHALINUS And the rest of the shoe – to kick you in the teeth, you evil old man!

OLYMPIO Would you like some tongue?

LYSIDAMUS I'm not inviting my wife!

OLYMPIO Once I'm at the market, I'll see what there is.

LYSIDAMUS Fair enough, now on your way. Don't skimp – buy plenty. Now my job is to see my neighbour Alcesimus, to make sure he's playing his part.

OLYMPIO I'll be off now, then.

LYSIDAMUS Yes

(*Exit* Olympio *along the street.* Lysidamus *knocks on the door of Alcesimus' house and: Exit* Lysidamus *into Alcesimus' house.*)

CHALINUS (*coming into the open*) Not even if I were offered my freedom three times over, would I miss the opportunity of landing these two in the soup! My mistress shall certainly be made fully aware of their plans. I have caught my enemies in the act; and if my mistress is willing to play her part, the day will be mine! How beautifully I'll catch them with their defences down! The omens are favourable: and now the conquered shall conquer! I'll go indoors now: ....and the food which is being spiced in one way will be spiced in quite another: and the dish that was being prepared for a certain person will not be prepared: but a dish will be prepared for a certain person which he was not expecting.

(*Exit* Chalinus *into Lysidamus' house.*)

ACT 3

(*Enter* Lysidamus *and* Alcesimus *from Alcesimus' house.*)

LYSIDAMUS I am now to find out whether you deserve a
verdict of friend or foe, Alcesimus. The evidence is
to be examined and the case is to be decided.
Now I have a list of banned words and phrases,
which I would ask you not to use. Such phrases as
'Why are you having an affair?' – put that on the list.
'With your white hair', 'At your time of life' – add
them to the list. 'You have a wife already' –
definitely put that on the list.
ALCESIMUS I've never seen anyone more head over heels
than you.
LYSIDAMUS Make sure your house is empty.
ALCESIMUS It will be! I've arranged to send all the slaves
and maids round to your house.
LYSIDAMUS Oh what a very fine fellow you are. But
make sure they hurry up. Remember not to let them
hang around at your house finishing off jobs.
ALCESIMUS I'll remember.
LYSIDAMUS Well, I can think of no finer man than you.
Take care.
I'm off into town now, but I'll be back soon.
ALCESIMUS Have a pleasant walk.
LYSIDAMUS By the way, does your house have a hair
brush?
ALCESIMUS Why?
LYSIDAMUS Because we want to be 'well-combed' into
your house (*laughs at his own joke*)
ALCESIMUS Oh dear. You need to be cut down to size –
you're enjoying yourself too much.

LYSIDAMUS But what's the point of being in love if I
    can't be clever and witty?
    Anyway, you just make sure I don't have to come
    looking for you.
ALCESIMUS I'll be at home.

(*Exeunt* Lysidamus *down the street and* Alcesimus *into his
house. Then*: *Enter* Cleostrata *from Lysidamus' house*)

[3.2]
CLEOSTRATA So then, this was why my husband was so
    eager for me to hurry up and invite my neighbour
    round – so that the house next door would be free for
    them to take Casina to. Well, I certainly won't be
    inviting her round now! I'm not creating empty
    houses for them, the old mutton-heads!

(*Enter* Alcesimus *from his doorway. He looks puzzled.*)

CLEOSTRATA But here comes our neighbour, that pillar of
    the Senate, that guardian of the People, who empties
    his house for the use of my husband. Well now, I
    wouldn't pay the price of a pinch of salt for him!
ALCESIMUS It's odd that my wife hasn't been invited next
    door yet: she's been dressed up and waiting for some
    time now. Ah, but here comes the invitation now, I
    suppose. Good afternoon, Cleostrata.
CLEOSTRATA Good afternoon, Alcesimus; and where is
    your wife?
ALCESIMUS Inside, waiting for you to invite her round.
    Your husband asked me to send her round to help
    you. Do you want me to call her?
CLEOSTRATA Oh no, let her be. It doesn't matter, if she's
    busy.

ALCESIMUS No, she's not doing anything special.

CLEOSTRATA No no, I don't want to be a nuisance.

ALCESIMUS But aren't you getting ready for a wedding round at your place?

CLEOSTRATA Yes we are.

ALCESIMUS Well, don't you need some help?

CLEOSTRATA Oh, I've enough help at home. I'll meet up with your wife when the wedding's over.
Well, goodbye for now and give my regards to your wife.

(*Exit* Cleostrata *into Lysidamus' house*)

ALCESIMUS What am I going to do now? I've got myself into a pickle here after that toothless old goat of a next door neighbour roped me into his hare-brained plans. Here am I offering for my wife to go round and give a helping hand, and she's not wanted. It's his own fault: he said his wife would ask her across; but she said it didn't matter. By the Gods, it's a wonder this next door neighbour of mine hasn't smelt a rat! On the other hand, when I think the matter over, if she had, I've a feeling she'd have made that clear! Oh well, I may as well go back in and drop anchor for a while.

(*Exit* Alcesimus *into his house.*
Then: Enter Cleostrata *from Lysidamus' house.*)

CLEOSTRATA Ha! Now that's made a fool of him! I like to see these poor old men in such a state! All we need now is for my useless decrepit old husband to come along and then I can make a fool of him as well.

Perhaps I can get the two of them into an argument between themselves.

(*looking down the street*) And here comes my husband now – and to look at his po-faced expression, you'd think he were an honourable man.

(*Cleostrata stands in the doorway*:
Enter Lysidamus *along the street.*)

[3.3]

LYSIDAMUS It is the height of folly, if you ask me, for a man who is in love to journey into town on business on the very day that his loved one is waiting in readiness for him.

I have just committed this act of folly. I have wasted the entire day in a lawsuit, acting for a relative of mine. That he lost his case, is, by Hercules, a source of great joy to me, in that he will not ask me to represent him in one of his hopeless cases again in a hurry.

Now it is my considered opinion, that the appointment of a lawyer to act in a case, should be preceded by close questioning of that lawyer as to whether he has his mind on the matter in hand. The lawyer who admits he has not, should be dismissed – freeing his mind to be engaged elsewhere.

(*noticing Cleostrata*) Oh no! That's my wife in the doorway!

Unfortunately, she's not deaf and will have heard everything I've said.

CLEOSTRATA I did hear everything you've said and you will regret it!

LYSIDAMUS I'll approach her.

What are you doing, my dearest?

53

CLEOSTRATA I was waiting for you.

LYSIDAMUS Are the preparations ready? Have you invited your neighbour round to help you?

CLEOSTRATA Oh yes. I invited her as you instructed.
But your comrade, (*pointing to Alcesimus' house*) your best friend, seems to have upset his wife in some way or other. He refused to allow his wife to come when I invited her.

LYSIDAMUS That's the trouble with you – you don't use any feminine charm.

CLEOSTRATA There are women, of a certain sort, who use their feminine charms on other women's husbands, dear husband, as you well know; but not respectably married women such as myself. Go and fetch her yourself! I'm going indoors as there are a number of things I need to take care of.

LYSIDAMUS Hurry up then.

CLEOSTRATA All right.
(*aside*) I'll put the fear of the Gods in him! He'll be in a pretty sorry love-sick state before today's out.

(*Exit* Cleostrata *into Lysidamus' house. Then:*
Enter Alcesimus *from his house.*)

[3.4]

ALCESIMUS Now, has our lover returned from town yet – making such fools of me and my wife! Ah, there he is, by his door.
(*to Lysidamus, angrily*) By Hercules, you're just the man I want to see!

LYSIDAMUS (*equally angrily*) And, by Hercules, you're just the man I want to see! What have you to say for yourself, you useless object? What job did I give you? What did I ask you to do?

54

ALCESIMUS Yes, what?!

LYSIDAMUS To provide me with an empty house. To send your wife round here to us. You've really put an end to my chances now, haven't you?

ALCESIMUS Go hang yourself! You were the one who said your wife would invite my wife round.

LYSIDAMUS Yes, and she says she did invite her round, but that you wouldn't let her come!

ALCESIMUS What?! She told me she didn't need her help!

LYSIDAMUS What?! It was her who told me to ask her!

ALCESIMUS What?! That's nonsense!

LYSIDAMUS Nonsense? What?! You're the one who's ruined everything!

ALCESIMUS Ruined everything! What?! Perhaps that's as well: you clearly deserve all you get.

LYSIDAMUS What?! What about you? You're not going to say 'What?!' more than me today!

ALCESIMUS What?! By Hercules, may the Gods destroy you!

LYSIDAMUS Right then: are you going to send your wife round, or not?

ALCESIMUS You take her round! And if you and your wife and that girlfriend of yours come to a sticky end, don't blame me!
(*calming down*) All right, you go and deal with something else, whilst I tell my wife to go through the garden round to your wife.

LYSIDAMUS Now you're a real friend – a brother in fact.

(*Exit* Alcesimus *into his house.*)

LYSIDAMUS Did I fail to see some bad omen when I entered into this affair of mine? And what have I ever

55

done to offend Venus, that she should put obstacles in my way at every turn?

(*Shouting is heard from within Lysidamus' house.*)

LYSIDAMUS What on earth is that din coming from our house?

[3.5]
(*Enter* Pardalisca *from Lysidamus' house, melodramatically overacting, pretending to be in a panic.*)

PARDALISCA Help! We are all undone! Oh help! I don't think my heart will stand all this! And my legs will not stop trembling! Help! I need somewhere to hide, somewhere to run! Where on earth can I get help? I've never seen the like! Inside! Such behaviour as this I've never witnessed before!
(*calling back through the door*) Be careful, Cleostrata! Keep well away from her before she does you some injury! Get the sword off her! She's gone mad! She doesn't know what she's doing!

LYSIDAMUS What's happened? Why is she out here frightened out of her mind? Pardalisca!

PARDALISCA (*continues to overact throughout*) I am dead! But whence do my ears perceive a sound?

LYSIDAMUS Look over here! It's me.

PARDALISCA Oh my master!

LYSIDAMUS What's wrong? What's frightening you?

PARDALISCA I am dead!

LYSIDAMUS Dead?

PARDALISCA Dead! And you are dead!

LYSIDAMUS Dead? How so?

PARDALISCA Beware!

56

LYSIDAMUS It seems you should beware.

PARDALISCA Hold me up: I'm going to fall.

LYSIDAMUS (*supporting her*) Whatever it is, tell me quickly!

PARDALISCA Hold my waist and fan me with your cloak.

LYSIDAMUS (*fans her*) This is all extremely worrying – (*suspiciously*) unless, of course, she's had a drop too much of the old vino.

PARDALISCA Please hold my ears.

LYSIDAMUS Don't be ridiculous: 'Hold my waist!' 'Hold my ears!'
Now, unless you tell me what this is all about, and quickly, I'll knock your silly brains out, my girl. D'you think you can take me for a fool?

PARDALISCA My master..

LYSIDAMUS My girl, what do you want of me?

PARDALISCA To be less angry.

LYSIDAMUS You're speaking out of turn. Tell me what's wrong – but be brief. What was that din inside?

PARDALISCA Listen and I'll tell you. It was the most dreadful thing – in our house – that slave-girl of yours started up as you've just heard – with behaviour quite contrary to what one expects in Athens...

LYSIDAMUS Go on.

PARDALISCA I'm so afraid, I can't use my tongue.

LYSIDAMUS If you don't loosen it, I will.

PARDALISCA Your girl, you know, the one you want to marry your farm manager – well, she was inside....

LYSIDAMUS Yes – inside - go on!

PARDALISCA Well, she put on a most disgraceful show, and began to threaten her own husband.
His life...

LYSIDAMUS (*alarmed*) What about his life?

57

PARDALISCA We-ell…

LYSIDAMUS Go on.

PARDALISCA She said she wanted to take his life. And the sword…

LYSIDAMUS (*again alarmed*) What!

PARDALISCA The sword….

LYSIDAMUS What sword?

PARDALISCA Which she held…

LYSIDAMUS By the Gods, why was she holding a sword?

PARDALISCA She was chasing everyone through the house. She wouldn't let anyone near her.
Everyone's hiding in the cellars or under the beds – they're all scared stiff.

LYSIDAMUS This has ruined everything! What on earth's come over her so suddenly?

PARDALISCA She's gone mad.

LYSIDAMUS I've heard of being unlucky, but really..!

PARDALISCA Well, if you were to hear what she's been saying today…

LYSIDAMUS I need to hear: what has she been saying?

PARDALISCA (*still melodramatic*) Listen. She swore by all the Gods and Goddesses that she would kill the man she sleeps with tonight.

LYSIDAMUS She's going to kill me?

PARDALISCA (*no longer overacting*) Why would she kill you?

LYSIDAMUS Ah..

PARDALISCA What did you say she had to do with you?

LYSIDAMUS Nothing. I meant to say 'Is she going to kill my farm manager?'

PARDALISCA Just a slip of the tongue, then?

LYSIDAMUS She's not threatening me, then?

PARDALISCA She's ranting about you more than anyone else.

58

LYSIDAMUS What for?

PARDALISCA Because you insisted she marry Olympio, and she's not going to allow you or her or her husband to remain alive until tomorrow.

I've been sent here to tell you to watch out for her.

LYSIDAMUS By Hercules, this is disastrous!

PARDALISCA (*aside*) Serves you right.

LYSIDAMUS (*aside*) Is anyone as unlucky in love as an old man like me?

PARDALISCA (*to the audience*) I seem to have him nicely fooled. My whole story is, of course, untrue: my mistress and her from next-door have set a trap, and my job is to make sure he falls into it!

LYSIDAMUS Er.. Pardalisca.

PARDALISCA Yes?

LYSIDAMUS There's something….

PARDALISCA Yes?

LYSIDAMUS There's something I want to ask you…

PARDALISCA You're beginning to delay me. (*turning to go*)

LYSIDAMUS And you're beginning to annoy me!

(*suddenly nervous*) But does Casina still have the sword?

PARDALISCA She does. Two of them in fact. She says she'll kill you with one and the farm manager with the other, today.

LYSIDAMUS I'm suffering death more times than any man alive!

I'd better look out my armour and put on my leather tunic. Now where's my wife? I think she put my armour away.

PARDALISCA No-one dares go near her.

LYSIDAMUS Can't someone speak nicely to her?

PARDALISCA We've tried. But she says she's not going to put them down at all, until she's certain she's not going to be married to your farm manager.

LYSIDAMUS Does she now? Well, in that case, she'll be married against her will. Why shouldn't I carry out my plan to have her marry me – er, that is – my farm manager?

PARDALISCA Another small slip of the tongue?

LYSIDAMUS Nervousness is affecting my speech. Now, I beg you, tell my wife that I'm asking her to persuade Casina to put down the swords and allow me to go back inside.

PARDALISCA I'll tell her. (*setting off indoors, but stopping again each time Lysidamus speaks*)

LYSIDAMUS And you speak to Casina, as well.

PARDALISCA I will.

LYSIDAMUS And speak nicely to her, as I know you can; d'you hear?

And if you persuade her, I'll be most grateful: in fact, I'll give you some sandals and a gold ring for your finger and lots of other things.

PARDALISCA I'll do my best.

LYSIDAMUS Make sure you do.

PARDALISCA Perhaps if you were to let me get on with it.

LYSIDAMUS Go and take care.

(*Exit* Pardalisca *into Lysidamus' house. Lysidamus looks along the street.*)

LYSIDAMUS Ah, at last. Here comes my assistant in all this, with the food for the wedding…

(*Enter* Olympio *and* Citrio *along the street with boxes etc. of food and*:
Enter Pardalisca, Cleostrata *and* Myrrhina *from Lysidamus' house, to help Olympio and Citrio.*)

LYSIDAMUS …and he has a train of helpers.

[3.6]
OLYMPIO (*to Citrio*) Come on, you time-waster, we haven't got all day!
CITRIO All right! We're doing our best.
OLYMPIO Well, if that's your best, you'll never get the food cooked!
And look at me when I'm talking to you!
CITRIO I can't look at you and talk to you at the same time – I'd walk into this door!
OLYMPIO Just hurry up.
CITRIO I don't know who you think you are.
OLYMPIO You'll soon find out who the slaves are around here.

(Pardalisca, Cleostrata *and* Myrrhina *take most of the food into Lysidamus' house. Citrio picks up some of the remaining food and takes it in.*)

OLYMPIO As for me, I'll soon be dressing up magnificently like a Roman patrician when I go to meet my master.
LYSIDAMUS Is everything going well, my fine fellow?
OLYMPIO It is.
LYSIDAMUS What's happening, then?
OLYMPIO You are in love; I'm hungry and thirsty.
LYSIDAMUS You seem to be being taken good care of.

OLYMPIO (*putting on airs*) Indeed, today my life enters a
  new stage.
LYSIDAMUS Just a minute! Don't overdo it.
OLYMPIO (*pretending to wave away a foul smell*) Ugh!
  Your conversation brings an offensive smell!
LYSIDAMUS What!
OLYMPIO Oh, are you still there?
  You are becoming somewhat troublesome.
LYSIDAMUS (*becoming increasingly angry*) I'll give you
  something much more than 'somewhat troublesome',
  unless you stop this!
OLYMPIO By Zeus, are you going to leave me now, or do
  you want me to vomit?
LYSIDAMUS Just a moment!
OLYMPIO What is it?
  (*looking contemptuously at Lysidamus*) Who is this
  man?
LYSIDAMUS I am your master!
OLYMPIO My master?
LYSIDAMUS Yes, you're my slave.
OLYMPIO A slave? I?
LYSIDAMUS Yes, mine.
OLYMPIO Am I not now a free man? You were setting me
  free. You do remember, don't you?
LYSIDAMUS (*unable to offend Olympio at this juncture*)
  Wait a moment, yes I do (*putting his hand on
  Olympio's shoulder*).
OLYMPIO Remove your hand, if you please.
LYSIDAMUS (*removing his hand*) It is I who am your
  slave.
OLYMPIO That's right.
LYSIDAMUS Olympio, my most caring patron!
OLYMPIO Correct!
LYSIDAMUS I am yours indeed!

OLYMPIO So what do I want with a worthless slave like
you?
LYSIDAMUS What indeed?

(*Enter* Citrio *and* Pardalisca *from Lysidamus' house. They go
about picking up the remaining food.*)

LYSIDAMUS How soon will you be able to reform me?
OLYMPIO As soon as dinner is cooked!
LYSIDAMUS (*in command again*) Hurry them up, then.
OLYMPIO (*to Citrio and Pardalisca*) Quickly! Hurry
indoors! Come on, get a move on!

(*Citrio is unable to work and be spoken to at the same time.
He stops to listen.*)

OLYMPIO I shall be in soon and I shall want a dinner
which will be drunkenly rich! Make it tasty and
special: I don't want any of that tasteless foreign
stuff!
(*to Citrio*) What are you standing there for?
Go on in: don't wait for me!

(*Exeunt* Pardalisca *and* Citrio *into Lysidamus' house with
remainder of food.*)

OLYMPIO (*to Lysidamus*) Nothing else to delay us, is
there?
LYSIDAMUS There's Casina with her sword. She's
supposed to be ready to kill me – and you.
OLYMPIO I know. So what? It's all nonsense. I know what
a bad lot these women are. You just go into the house
with me.
LYSIDAMUS By the gods, I think there'll be trouble.

You go first and see what's going on indoors.
OLYMPIO My life's as dear to me as yours is to you.
You go first.
LYSIDAMUS If you say so. Well er.. I'll go …with you.

(*Exeunt* Lysidamus *and* Oympio *into Lysidamus' house,*
each pushing the other to enter first.)

ACT 4

(Enter Pardalisca *from Lysidamus' house)*

PARDALISCA   Well, well! I don't believe the Games at
Nemea, nor the Olympic Games, nor any other
games, have been as lively as the games being played
in this house *(indicating Lysidamus' house)*: and
they're all having great fun at the expense of the old
man and Olympio our farm manager!
The whole house is bustling with the wedding
preparations and the old man's in the kitchen urging
on the cooks: 'Are you going to do anything, today?'
he says, 'Is there going to be any food? Hurry up; the
dinner should have been cooked by now!'.
Meanwhile, the farm manager is strolling about, with
a garland on his head, washed and decked out in his
white wedding outfit.
Cleostrata and her neighbour Myrrhina are in a
bedroom, dressing up the slave Chalinus in the guise
of Casina as the bride to be married to Olympio. And
what a brilliant show they put on – as if they didn't
know what's going to come of all this.
And the cooks are doing a fine job, putting all their
energy into ensuring the old man gets no dinner
whatsoever: they're knocking over the pots, spilling
water onto the fires, doing anything the two ladies
want them to. And the two ladies are doing their
utmost to drive the old man out of the house without
any dinner: they want to fill themselves up with food
without him around: and they can eat a barge-load of
food, those two old dustbins!

(Lysidamus' house door begins to open)

65

PARDALISCA Ah! The door's opening.

(*Enter* Lysidamus *through the door.*)

[4.2]
LYSIDAMUS (*Already drunk, he holds a wine flask. He speaks to Cleostrata within*) Cleostrata, I think you would be wise to dine as soon as the dinner is ready. I shall have dined at the farm. I wish to accompany the new bride and her new groom to the farm: after all, there may be someone around who's up to no good. We don't want anyone abducting the bride, do we?

Now you have a good time. But hurry up and send the young man and young lady out quickly so that we can reach the farm before it's dark. I shall be back tomorrow and I can enjoy my share of the feast then.

PARDALISCA (*aside*) It's happening just as I said: the women have evicted the old man without his dinner.

LYSIDAMUS (*sees Pardalisca*) What are you doing here?

PARDALISCA I'm on an errand for my mistress.

LYSIDAMUS Is that so?

PARDALISCA It is, truly.

LYSIDAMUS You're spying, aren't you?

PARDALISCA No, not at all.

LYSIDAMUS On your way! Don't hang around here, while everyone else is busy inside.

PARDALISCA I'm going (*moves slowly to Lysidamus' door*)

LYSIDAMUS Well go on then, you useless female!

(*Exit* Pardalisca *into Lysidamus' house.*)

LYSIDAMUS Has she gone? Now I can speak freely. I am
 going without my dinner. Do I care? No! I am in
 love!
 (*looking down the street*) But look who comes here.
 Wearing his garland and his wedding outfit, here
 comes my ally, my partner, my co-bridegroom,
 Olympio.

(*Enter* Olympio *along the street. He has acquired a laurel
wreath to add to his white wedding tunic. He also holds a
wine flask, out of which he has clearly been drinking.*)

[4.3]
OLYMPIO If they don't bring my new bride outdoors soon,
 we'll have to sing the wedding song without her.
LYSIDAMUS How are you, my Hope and Salvation?
OLYMPIO I'm starving, by Hercules, and there's no hope
 and salvation in that!
LYSIDAMUS Ah, but I am in love.
OLYMPIO Well, you're all right then, if you can live off
 love. As for me, my stomach's empty and it's been
 rumbling for some time now.
LYSIDAMUS Yes, I don't know how they've managed to
 waste so much time in there. It's as if they're doing it
 on purpose: the more I hurry them on, the less they
 achieve.
OLYMPIO What if I start the wedding song?
 D'you think that will speed them up?
LYSIDAMUS Good idea! It's a joint wedding so I'll join in
 with you.
LYSIDAMA ⎫   (*chanting*)
                  ⎬   Hymen, God of Marriage! Hymen O!
OLYMPIO   ⎭

LYSIDAMAS This is a disaster. Do you think she's going to come soon? I'm ready to come now! (*Lysidamus and Olympio both laugh drunkenly.*)

OLYMPIO Eh! This waiting around is becoming more and more difficult for you.

LYSIDAMUS Why's that?

OLYMPIO Well, it's getting hard already!

(Lysidamus *and* Olympio *again laugh drunkenly. Then Lysidamus' door begins to open.*)

OLYMPIO At last, the door's opening: they're coming out.

LYSIDAMUS By Hercules, the Gods are on my side after all!

(*Enter* Pardalisca, Chalinus *dressed as a bride and wearing a white veil,* Cleostrata *and* Myrrhina *through Lysidamus' door.*)

[4.4]

CHALINUS (*aside – raising his veil*) Here's the Casina they've picked up the scent of. (*replacing his veil.*)

PARDALISCA (*standing close to Chalinus, she speaks as if pronouncing a formal prayer*) Gently now, my new bride, lift your feet clear over the threshold…

(*Chalinus steps over the threshold.*)

…so as to be safe and sound at the beginning of this, your journey. May you outlive your husband; may you dominate him, conquer him and remain victorious over him; may your words be obeyed and your house be your empire; may your husband provide all and may you take all; may you deceive your husband, night and day. Remember this, I pray.

OLYMPIO By Hercules, she'll regret saying all that, the moment she steps out of line!

LYSIDAMUS Be quiet!

OLYMPIO I won't be quiet.

LYSIDAMUS What's wrong with you?

OLYMPIO That girl makes me mad.

LYSIDAMUS But you're making my carefully prepared plans unprepared. That's what they're trying to do; that's what they want – to undo what I've done.

PARDALISCA Come, Olympio, when you will; receive from us this woman as your wife.

OLYMPIO Give her to me then, if you're going to give her to me at all today.

LYSIDAMUS Yes, very good. Now all of you: go inside, please. (*He is ignored*)

PARDALISCA (*to Olympio*) Please be gentle with this chaste and inexperienced girl.

OLYMPIO I will be.

PARDALISCA Farewell!

OLYMPIO (*to the women*) Go now.

LYSIDAMUS Yes, go inside.

PARDALISCA Now farewell!

(*Exeunt* Cleostrata, Myrrhina *and* Pardalisca *into Lysidamus' house.*)

LYSIDAMUS Has my wife left yet?

OLYMPIO Yes, she's in the house; don't worry.

LYSIDAMUS Yes!! Now, by the Gods, I'm free at last!

(*In a drunken attempt at tenderness, Lysidamus holds out his arms to Chalinus, still holding his wine flask.*)

LYSIDAMUS   My sweetheart, my honey-bun, my little
   spring flower.
OLYMPIO (*fiercely intervening*) `Ey you! I'd be careful, if
   I were you. She's mine!
LYSIDAMUS I know, but I'm to pick the first fruit.
OLYMPIO Here, you hold this wine flask.
LYSIDAMUS (*refusing*) No thank you; I'll hold this little
   one instead.
   (*stands by Chalinus.*)
   Mighty Venus, you gave me a great gift when you
   gave me this treasure.
OLYMPIO (*forcing Lysidamus out of the way and putting
   his arm round Chalinus*) Ah, my little wife, my
   dearest one.

(*Chalinus stamps on Olympio's foot.*)

OLYMPIO Ah!
LYSIDAMUS What happened?
OLYMPIO   She stamped on me like one of Hannibal's
   elephants!
LYSIDAMUS   Never mind! There is no cloud so soft as
   these breasts…
OLYMPIO Indeed, they are beautiful…

(*Chalinus   flicks   his   elbow   into   Olympio's   chest,
accompanied by thudding sound.*)

OLYMPIO Ouch!
LYSIDAMUS What's wrong?
OLYMPIO She elbowed me in the chest. I say 'elbowed': it
   was more like a battering ram.

LYSIDAMUS You're far too rough, you know. Now me, I
    treat her with gentleness. (*putting his arm round
    Chalinus*) See: she's not declaring war on me.

(*Olympio approaches; Chalinus flicks his elbow into his
face, accompanied by thudding sound.*)

OLYMPIO Ah!
LYSIDAMUS What's the matter?
OLYMPIO Well, she's a powerful little thing. Nearly put
    me on my back with that elbow.
LYSIDAMUS Obviously wants to be on her back herself!
OLYMPIO Let's go in then.
LYSIDAMUS Come in, my dear.

(*Exeunt* Chalinus, Olympio *and* Lysidamus *into Alcesimus'
house.*)

ACT 5

(*Enter* Cleostrata, Myrrhina *and* Pardalisca *from Lysidamus' house. They are laughing at the trick they have played on Lysidamus and Olympio.*)

MYRRHINA We've been well wined and dined indoors: so here we are out in the street to watch the marriage games. I haven't had such a good laugh for a long time, and I don't think I will for some time to come.

PARDALISCA I'd like to know what Chalinus is doing – newly married with his new husband!

MYRRHINA You know, I think our playwright has come up with quite a neat trick here.

CLEOSTRATA I'd like to see that old husband of mine come out with a black eye.
Your husband is a disgrace for giving him the use of your house, but my husband must be the biggest disgrace alive! Now, Pardalisca, I want you to keep guard here to make sure that whoever comes out of that door receives appropriate ridicule from us all.

PARDALISCA I'd be delighted.

(*Myrrhina and Cleostrata make sure Pardalisca is in a hidden but suitable place to see Alcesimus' door, and then withdraw slightly further off.*)

MYRRHINA Watch carefully from here and tell us what's going on.

PARDALISCA I think I'm all right here.

MYRRHINA Yes, don't be afraid: tell us everything that happens.

(*Alcesimus' door begins to open.*)

PARDALISCA Quiet! The door's opening.

[5.2]
(*Enter* Olympio *from Alcesimus' door. He doesn't come fully onto stage at first, but peers round the doorway to see if anyone is there. He sports a black eye and is extremely embarrassed. He is so unsure of himself that he at first retreats back into Alcesimus' house and shuts the door. He re-emerges and come out into the open. He looks shiftily about himself. His clothes are dishevelled. His embarrassment is obvious.*)

OLYMPIO Where to run? Where to hide? How to hide our
    shame? This 'marriage' of ours will plunge my
    master and me into such depths of humiliation that I
    fear ridicule is all that will remain for both of us!
    This venture of mine was foolish and the price is
    shame.
        (*to the audience*) You might as well listen to my tale
    – it's certainly a ridiculously sorry one. I lead my
    new wife straight to a small room, as dark as a
    dungeon: I want to get in – as it were – before the old
    man. I am not short of soft coaxing talk: 'Lie down' I
    say. My advances are rejected. My cause is becoming
    (*looks uncomfortable*) more urgent. I fear the old
    man will interrupt us, so I lock the door....
MYRRHINA (*to Cleostrata*) Come on: you go up to him.
CLEOSTRATA (*approaching Olympio*) Excuse me;
    where's your new bride?
OLYMPIO I'm dead, by Hercules! The story's out!
CLEOSTRATA You might as well tell us all about it, then.
    What happened in there? How did Casina do?
    Everything went all right, did it?

73

OLYMPIO Er..well..

CLEOSTRATA Go on; tell us all about it – since you've started.

OLYMPIO Er..well..

CLEOSTRATA Come on.

You said 'Lie down'. Then what happened?

OLYMPIO Well, when I got very close to her, I discovered she had a sword hidden under her dress: I got hold of the hilt... it was warm... (*his voice fades*) at least I think it was a sword.

CLEOSTRATA Perhaps it wasn't a sword.

OLYMPIO Er..no..

CLEOSTRATA What was it?

OLYMPIO (*uncomfortably*) I don't know.

Whatever it was, it was certainly in fine fettle.

MYRRHINA (*coming forward to join Cleostrata*) What happened next? Do tell us.

OLYMPIO Well, I tried to kiss Casina...

MYRRHINA And what happened?

OLYMPIO I got a mouthful of bristly beard! And as I knelt, she gave me a hefty kick in the chest! While I fell off the bed, up she jumps and smacked me in the eye. Without a word, I fled the room and came out here, with my clothes splendidly arranged as you can see.

(*pauses*) And I've left the old man to drink from the same cup as I have!

CLEOSTRATA It's for the best! But where's your cloak?

OLYMPIO I've left it inside.

CLEOSTRATA Never mind! You have been led a merry dance, though, haven't you?

OLYMPIO (*seeing the joke and wishing to join in the joke on Lysidamus*) Yes, and I suppose we deserved it.

(*Alcesimus' door begins to open*)

74

OLYMPIO   The door's opening: she's not chasing me out here, is she?

(All *withdraw so that they cannot be readily seen from Alcesimus' doorway. Then: Enter* Lysidamus, *replicating Olympio's previous entry.*)

[5.3]
LYSIDAMUS   O-oh! My reputation is in flames and there's nothing I can do about it. How can I look my wife in the face? I'm done for! My conduct is for all to see. However you look at it, I'm as good as dead! Caught in the act, I have no way of excusing myself to my wife. A secret marriage! – I've even lost my cloak.
Oh well, I might as well go to Cleostrata, confess all and bare my back.

(*Cleostrata moves to be visible to the audience but not to Lysidamus, and looks particularly fierce. At her side stand Myrrhina and Pardalisca, both looking grim. Then: Enter* Citrio *carrying a whip, which he gives to Cleostrata; then Enter* Alcesimus *who stands by his door, looking worried and shame-faced.*)

LYSIDAMUS   (*to the audience, hopefully*) Perhaps there is a gentleman in the audience who would care to take my place?
(*waits, then disappointedly*) I thought not. What else can I do – unless I imitate a thieving slave and run away? I'll be beaten black and blue if I return home.

75

(*to the audience*) You all think I'm overdoing it, don't you? Well, I'm not, I can assure you. You should see my wife when she loses her temper!

(*Enter* Chalinus *quietly through Alcesimus' door. He is not noticed by Lysidamus*)

LYSIDAMUS On the whole, I think the most sensible plan is to clear off!

(*Lysidamus sets off down the street.*)

[5.4]
CHALINUS Hey! Not so fast, my young lover!
LYSIDAMUS Oh no, That voice! I'll carry on as if I haven't heard.
CHALINUS (*sharply*) Where do you think you're going?

(*Lysidamus freezes.*)

CHALINUS Off to some more love-making, are you – in the Gallic style?
Now if you want to return to bed, now's your chance. Please, let's return to our room.
(*suddenly threatening*) By Hercules you'll pay for it! Come on! (*indicating Alcesimus' house*) This way! I have a fair judge (*indicating his fist*) who doesn't sit in court!
LYSIDAMUS Clearly, unless I want a punch where it hurts, I'd better continue in this direction (*indicating down the street*), whilst back there could be extremely painful!

(*Lysidamus attempts to continue along the street, but Cleostrata comes forward and intercepts him.*)

CLEOSTRATA Hello, my young lover!
LYSIDAMUS Out of the frying pan into the fire – it's my
    wife! But the frying pan had a large fist – the proverb
    didn't mention that.
    (*facing Cleostrata*) Perhaps the fire will be easier to
    deal with.

(*Myrrhina joins Cleostrata.*)

MYRRHINA What do you think you're doing, you double-
    crossing husband?
CLEOSTRATA Yes, my husband, how have you got into
    such a state? And where's your cloak?
MYRRHINA I think he's been too busy with Casina to
    think about his cloak.
LYSIDAMUS I'm ruined!
CHALINUS Are you coming back to bed then, with me,
    your Casina?
LYSIDAMUS Clear off!
CHALINUS You mean you don't love me?!
CLEOSTRATA So tell me, what did happen to your cloak?
LYSIDAMUS Er... There were some Bacchanalian
    revellers ... (*laughs nervously*)
CLEOSTRATA Bacchanalian revellers?
LYSIDAMUS Yes, revellers – honouring Bacchus...
MYRRHINA He's talking nonsense and he knows it!
    There aren't any Bacchanalian revels at the moment.
LYSIDAMUS Oh yes, I forgot that. However, some
    Bacchanalian revellers ...
CLEOSTRATA Bacchanalian revellers?

LYSIDAMUS   Er...well...er... if there aren't any round here...er..
CLEOSTRATA By the Gods, you're panicking!
LYSIDAMUS Me?
CLEOSTRATA And you're lying, by Hercules, and you've gone pale. Don't try to make excuses: we understood your plan from the outset. Chalinus here is our Casina and what a fool he's made out of you!

(*Olympio comes forward.*)

CLEOSTRATA   You didn't even treat Olympio here fairly...
OLYMPIO   No, my reputation's in ruins thanks to his deceitfulness.
LYSIDAMUS (*to Olympio*) Can't you be quiet?
OLYMPIO No, by Hercules, I can't be quiet! You begged me over and over again to ask to marry Casina – all to help a love affair for yourself.
LYSIDAMUS (*feigning incredulity*) I did that?
OLYMPIO No, it was Hector of Troy.
LYSIDAMUS (*angrily*) Never mind Hector of Troy!
(*incredulous again*) Did I really do what you say I did?
CLEOSTRATA Are you really asking us?
LYSIDAMUS (*nearly contrite*) Well, *if* I did as you say, I was in the wrong.
CLEOSTRATA   Come back inside here (*indicating Lysidamus' house*).
If you can't remember, I can rectify any memory loss.
LYSIDAMUS By Hercules, I'd better believe what you say. But Cleostrata, my wife, (*sinking to his knees*) pardon your husband. Myrrhina, beg her on my behalf. If

78

ever I show, or even begin to show, any interest in Casina after this, you will have every right to have me hung up and soundly flogged.

MYRRHINA I think that perhaps you should pardon him.

CLEOSTRATA I will do as you say. I pardon you, husband, without further debate – otherwise this play will go on all night.

LYSIDAMUS You are not angry?

CLEOSTRATA I am not angry

LYSIDAMUS You give me your word?

CLEOSTRATA You have my word.

LYSIDAMUS No man ever had a more wonderful wife than I!

(Lysidamus stands up again and takes Cleostrata's hand.)

CLEOSTRATA *(to Chalinus)* Come on – give him his cloak back.

(Chalinus quickly retrieves Lysidamus' cloak from Alcesimus' house and gives it to Lysidamus.)

CHALINUS Take it if you want it.
    (to the audience) But I seem to have suffered a remarkable hurt: I've been married to two men at the same time – and neither of them gave me what a young bride expects!

(Exeunt Cleostrata, Lysidamus *and* Pardalisca *into Lysidamus' house,* Myrrhina *and* Alcesimus *into Alcesimus' house, and* Olympio, Citrio *and* Chalinus *along the street.)*

EPILOGUE

Gentle audience, our play now draws to a close and it remains for me to tell you how the story ends.

It will soon be discovered that Casina is in fact the long-lost daughter of our next-door neighbours (*indicating Alcesimus' house*). She was stolen as a baby and her whereabouts were unknown. Being Alcesimus' daughter, she is a full, free citizen of Athens.

She will soon fall in love with and marry Euthynicus, the son of my master, and, of course, they will live happily ever after.

Audience, farewell. May *your* secret affairs be more successful than this one, and may *we* now receive your applause!

.